The
Rosary

Nicholas King SJ

kevin
mayhew

For DHK,
with the undoubted encouragement
of your patron saint

Contents

The Rosary Explained

Welcome to this ancient form of prayer, which is still very much alive today. We do not know, as a matter of fact, how old it is. Traditionally, the Rosary (the word means a 'garland of roses') was ascribed to St Dominic (1170–1221), founder of the great Dominican order; and he was said to have used it as a weapon against the Albigensian heresy. Well, you can't use the Rosary as a weapon, and the idea of using a string of beads as a guide for reciting a prescribed number of prayers is much older than Dominic. In any case the idea of praying through the mysteries of the life of Jesus in this way cannot be dated to later than his time; the origin does not matter. What is important is that people have found it over the centuries an enormous help in their journey towards God.

For readers who are used to praying the Rosary, what is new about this book is that it provides you with the relevant scriptural texts, using my own translation (it is possible that you may find it fresher in certain respects than other versions with which you may be familiar). In addition, you will also find some comments, and occasionally questions, which are intended to help you pray through the relevant passages relating to the 20 mysteries of the Rosary. If you did not realise that there are now 20, not 15, mysteries, then you should read on; otherwise, you can go straight to the first joyful mystery. If, on the other hand, this way of prayer is unfamiliar to you, there may be one or two questions you would like to ask, such as the ones I have suggested below.

What do you do to 'say the Rosary'?

As I have said, it is a matter of praying through the mysteries of the life of Jesus. By 'mysteries', I do not mean the detective stories with which you beguile your leisure hours, but certain key moments in God's plan to rescue the human race. 'Mystery' here is not so much an apparently insoluble problem, more a stage in Jesus' life whose rich significance becomes more apparent the longer we reflect on it. The mysteries start and end, you will notice, with Mary, who said that first vital 'Yes' to the angel's invitation, and so became, astonishingly, the Mother of God.

Traditionally there were 15 such mysteries: five 'joyful', five 'sorrowful', and five 'glorious'. More recently, Pope John Paul II added the 'Mysteries of Light', so that at least some elements of the life of Jesus between his childhood and his death might be included in the prayer.

When do you say the Mysteries?

You can of course say them whenever you please; but there was a tradition of saying the Joyful Mysteries on Monday and Thursday, the Sorrowful on Tuesday and Friday, and the Glorious on Wednesday and Saturday (and Sunday, because seven can't be divided by three). When the 'Mysteries of Light' were introduced they were assigned to Thursday. But you could, for example, say just one of the mysteries each day. Something that I have discovered is that it is quite a good way of praying, on days when I have to travel in the early morning, and am unable to pray in my accustomed time and place.

What do you say when you pray the Rosary?

Traditionally, you start off by saying one Our Father and three Hail Marys, followed by the 'Glory be to the Father'. Don't worry if you don't know the words of these prayers; you will find them printed opposite. The idea here is to get into the mood of prayer before you start on the individual mysteries. Then to each mystery, you recite the Our Father once, followed by 10 Hail Marys, and finish with the Glory Be. Some people like to add the Apostles' Creed or to end with one of the great hymns to Mary that the Church has used for night prayer for a thousand years or more; but in this book we are just offering the simplest form of the Rosary.

Our Father

Our Father, who art in heaven,
hallowed be thy name;
thy kingdom come;
thy will be done on earth as it is in heaven.
Give us this day our daily bread;
and forgive us our trespasses,
as we forgive those who trespass against us;
and lead us not into temptation,
but deliver us from evil.
Amen.

Hail, Mary

Hail, Mary, full of grace,
the Lord is with thee.
Blessed art thou among women,
and blessed is the fruit of thy
womb, Jesus.
Holy Mary, Mother of God,
pray for us sinners, now,
and at the hour of our death.
Amen.

Glory Be

Glory be to the Father
and to the Son
and to the Holy Spirit,
as it was in the beginning,
is now, and ever shall be,
world without end.
Amen.

Isn't it all mumbo-jumbo?

Some people think that it is just a matter of reciting incantations like magic spells – the more you do it, the more powerful the magic. Try instead to think of the recitation of the words as creating in you a prayerful atmosphere from which you can consider the mystery on which you are praying, and relate it to your life.

In this book, you will find a suggested Scripture passage, drawn from my own translation of the New Testament, published by Kevin Mayhew. The idea is that the biblical text will focus your prayer on the particular stage of the life of Jesus on which you are reflecting; and I have added some comments or questions that may help you to pray. Alternatively, and this is something that I have found helpful, you might like simply to take a single phrase from the Scripture, and reflect on how that text fits the episode from Jesus' life that you are praying over.

Doesn't all this mean that you are worshipping the Virgin Mary?

No. But, as I have said, the Rosary begins with Mary (the appearance to her of the angel Gabriel), and ends with Mary (her Assumption into heaven and Coronation), as well as with us (The Glory of All the Saints). God's plan, astonishingly, depends on the co-operation of human beings, such as Mary, and such as ourselves. The Hail Mary is in fact a very ancient formula, consisting of, first, the angel's greeting, which you will find in the opening chapter of Luke's Gospel, and then a prayer, which uses Mary's very ancient title 'Mother of God', and asks her to intercede for us 'now' (for we always need prayers) and at that critical moment, 'the hour of our death'.

The point here is an important one. Almost as soon as Christians started to reflect on the mystery of Jesus, they realised that in order to talk accurately about him they had to speak of him not only as human but also as divine. And if that was so, then it was important to take seriously the reality of Mary from whom Jesus took his human flesh. So it was as early as the fifth century that Christians knew that they had to call her 'Mother of God', if they were to do justice to the truth about Jesus. That has been the position of most Christians in the history of Christianity. So, no, we do not worship Mary as God. We do however treasure her power of intercession (remembering how she persuaded her Son at the marriage-feast at Cana).

Final word

Enjoy (that is not too strong a word) this ancient method of praying. It is particularly useful for praying unobtrusively, especially while travelling. And it can be very relaxing, allowing the imagination to take over from our weary brain, and lead us up to God.

Nicholas King SJ

The Joyful Mysteries

The Annunciation

In the sixth month the angel Gabriel was sent to a city of Galilee whose name is Nazareth, to a virgin engaged to a man whose name was Joseph, of the house of David; and the name of the virgin was Mary.

And going in to her he said, 'Rejoice, you who have received favour: the Lord is with you.'

She was deeply disturbed at the remark, and wondered what kind of thing this greeting might be.

And the angel said to her, 'Do not be afraid, Mary. For you have found favour with God. And look! you will conceive in the womb, and bear a son. And you shall call his name Jesus. This one will be great, and will be called Son of the Most High. And the Lord will give him the throne of his ancestor David. And he shall rule over the house of David for ever and of his reign there shall be no end.'

And Mary said to the angel, 'How will this be, since I do not know a man?'

And the angel answered and said to her, '[The] Holy Spirit will come upon you, and the power of the Most High will overshadow you. Therefore that which is conceived is holy and will be called Son of God. And look, Elisabeth, your kinswoman, she too has conceived a son in her old age, and this is the sixth month for her who was called "Barren"; because there is no such thing as an impossibility to God.'

Mary said, 'Look, the Lord's slave-woman. Let it happen to me in accordance with your word.' And the angel went from her.

Luke 1:26-38

Gaze long at this lovely picture, which a thousand artists have tried to paint. Listen with Mary as she is instructed 'do not be afraid', and as she shares her difficulty with the angel: 'how will this be?'. Mary is utterly ready to go along with God's invitation. Notice how Mary, the girl of no status from an utterly insignificant village, is the main character in this scene. This is typical of the Gospel of Luke, for whom the

*least important names often turn out to be the ones who
matter. But there is more; for one character is not mentioned,
and yet underlies every line of the text, namely God.
Consider what Luke is saying when he says at the beginning
of this section, 'the angel Gabriel was sent': by whom? By,
clearly, God, who is in sole charge of all the events that Luke
narrates. That is something for us to remember in our
reading of Luke's Gospel. We watch in astonishment as
Mary accepts what God asks of her.*

The Visitation

Mary arose in those days and journeyed in a hurry to the
hill-country, to a city of Judah, and she entered the house of
Zachariah and greeted Elisabeth. And it happened when
Elisabeth heard Mary's greeting, the unborn child leapt in her
womb, and Elisabeth was filled with the Holy Spirit, and she
cried out in a loud voice and said, 'Blessed are you among
women, and blessed is the fruit of your womb. And how does
this happen to me, that the Mother of my Lord should come to
me? For look! as the sound of your greeting came to my ears,
the unborn child leapt with exultation in my womb. And happy
is she who believed that there would be a fulfilment of the
things spoken to her from the Lord.'

And Mary said,

> 'My soul extols the Lord
> and my spirit has exulted in God my Saviour
> because he has looked [favourably] on the humble state
> of his slave girl.
> For look! From now on, all generations will congratulate me
> because the Powerful One has done great things for me,
> and holy is his name.
> And his mercy is for generation after generation
> on those who fear him.
> He has done a mighty deed with his arm.
> He has scattered those who are haughty in the thoughts
> of their heart.
> He has deposed rulers from their thrones
> and raised up the humble.
> The hungry he has filled with good things
> and the wealthy he has sent away empty.
> He has helped his servant Israel, remembering his mercy.
> As he spoke to our ancestors,
> to Abraham and his descendants for ever.'

Mary remained with her about three months, and she returned to her home.

Luke 1:39-56

In this episode, with consummate artistry, Luke brings two stories, those of John the Baptist and Jesus, effortlessly together. Notice the two themes of 'journeying', and of

The Nativity

It came to pass in those days that a decree went out from
Caesar Augustus that the whole empire should be registered.
This, the first registration, took place when Quirinius was
governor of Syria. And everyone journeyed to be registered,
each to their own city. Joseph also went up from Galilee, from
the city of Nazareth, to Judaea, to the city of David which is
called Bethlehem, because he was of the house and family of
David, to be registered along with Mary, his betrothed – who
was pregnant. It came to pass while they were there that the
days were fulfilled for her to give birth and she brought forth
her son, the first-born; and she wrapped him round with
swathing-bands, and laid him down in a feeding-trough,
because there was no room for them in the lodging house.

And there were shepherds in the same region, who were living in the fields, and keeping careful watch by night over their flock. And the Angel of the Lord stood near them; and the glory of the Lord shone about them; and they feared with a great fear.

And the angel said to them, 'Do not be afraid. For look – I bring you good news, great joy which will be for all the people, that there has been born for you today a Saviour, who is Christ the Lord in the city of David; and this is the sign for you: you will find the baby wrapped in swathing-bands and lying in a feeding-trough.'

And suddenly there was with the angel a crowd of the heavenly army praising God and saying,

'Glory in the highest to God and on earth peace among human beings who are pleasing to God.'

Luke 2:1-14

This all-too-familiar passage is in certain respects a shocking one. It is far from the birth that we should expect of one who 'will be called great, and Son of the Most High', who will 'sit on the throne of his ancestor David', and 'will reign over the house of Jacob for ever, and of his reign there shall be no end'. The references to Caesar Augustus, the most powerful man in the world, and to Quirinius, his local representative, flatter only to deceive. These two potentates know nothing of Jesus, and their actions have the unforeseen consequence (unforeseen by them at any rate) that Jesus is born in Bethlehem. Not only that, but he is born in less than ideal circumstances: there is no room in the town's single lodging house, so the child is born like one of the poor and put in a 'feeding-trough'.

As a matter of fact, Luke has got his dates a bit muddled, since Quirinius was governor of Syria about ten years after Jesus was born, and we know nothing of the 'registration' of which Luke speaks. That, however, is not important. What matters to Luke is the contrast between the 'great ones' of the earth and the child that has been born.

Lastly, notice the shock of the reference to Mary's pregnancy. It is true that we already know the circumstances; nevertheless, the way Luke expresses it brings us up short.

The story of the shepherds confirms all that has gone before, including the superiority of Jesus over John the Baptist. There is also at least one shock, however; for the recipients of the vision are not, like Zachariah, Temple priests going about their business, nor, like Mary, quietly ready to do God's bidding; they are, frankly, cowboys, people living on the margins of society, and making up their rules as they go along, perhaps the very people that Luke's well-to-do Christians would have had least in common with. They live out of doors, and are not even respectable enough to sleep at nights.

Nevertheless, it is to these 'cowboys' that the Lord's revelation comes; and, remarkably, they do not hesitate to

believe, especially after the 'heavenly army' has sung a
chorus for them. This is of a piece with the (repeated) shock
that the 'Saviour, Christ the Lord' is currently lying in a
feeding-trough. Another repetition or echo is that, like Mary
earlier when she went rushing to visit Elisabeth, the
shepherds respond 'in a hurry'.

The Presentation in the Temple

And when the eight days were fulfilled for him to be circumcised, his name was called Jesus, which [he] had been called by the angel before he had been conceived in the womb.

And when the days of their purification were fulfilled according to the Law of Moses, they took him up to Jerusalem, to offer him to the Lord, as it is written in the Law of the Lord that 'every male that opens his mother's womb shall be called holy to the Lord', and to give sacrifice according to what is written in the Law of the Lord, 'a pair of turtle-doves, or two young doves'.

And look! There was a man in Jerusalem, whose name was Simeon, and this man was righteous and pious, and waiting for Israel's comfort; and the Holy Spirit was on him. And it had been revealed to him by the Holy Spirit [that he would not] see death before he saw the Christ of the Lord. And he came in the Spirit into the Temple; and as the parents brought in the child Jesus, for them to act in accordance with the Law about him, he himself took him into his arms and blessed God and said,

'Now you are letting your slave go, Master,
according to your word in peace;
because my eyes have seen your salvation
which you have prepared before the face of all the peoples,
a light for the revelation of the Gentiles
and the glory of your people Israel.'

And the child's father and mother were in a state of
astonishment at the things being said about him; and Simeon
blessed them, and said to Mary his mother: 'Look! This one is
destined for the fall and rising of many in Israel, and as a sign
of contradiction (and your own soul will be pierced by a sword)
so that the thoughts of many hearts may be revealed.'

Luke 2:22-35

*Luke here shows his skill in creating atmosphere. See how
subtly he emphasises that Jesus' parents observe the Law;
and this picture is reinforced by Simeon, who steps straight
out of the pages of the Old Testament. And it goes deeper.
Three times the Spirit is mentioned, for it is the Holy Spirit
who drives the story, according to Luke. Listen to Simeon's
song, which has been for a millennium and a half part of the
Church's night prayer, with its reference to 'revelation of the
Gentiles', along with 'glory of Israel'. Simeon sides with the
lowly, classing himself as a slave, just as Mary does.*

Above all, though, it is a central theme of Luke's Gospel that God is in charge; and this is indicated quite emphatically in the account of Jesus' circumcision, which is performed in accordance with God's Law, but also (and more specifically) in accordance with the instruction of the angel Gabriel to Mary. As before, we are invited to contemplate the meaning of the child, through the lens of his parents' 'astonishment' and Simeon's song of farewell. This is a powerful picture to meditate on.

One last point to notice is the theme, once more, of journeying. In the first two chapters of Luke the scene shifts no fewer than nine times, between Judaea and Galilee. The rest of the Gospel and Acts, its companion volume, is a journey driven by the Spirit.

The Finding in the Temple

And his parents used to journey each year to Jerusalem for the Passover festival. And when he was twelve years old, when they went up according to the custom of the feast, and when they had completed the days, as they returned, the boy Jesus stayed behind in Jerusalem; and his parents did not know. Thinking that he was in the caravan, they went a day's journey, and then started to hunt for him everywhere among their relatives and acquaintances; and when they couldn't find him, they returned to Jerusalem in their hunt for him; and so it was that after three days they found him sitting in the Temple in the middle of the teachers, and [he was] listening to them and asking them questions; and all those who heard him were astonished at his intellect and at his responses. And when they saw him they were overwhelmed; and his mother said to him, 'Child, why did you do this to us? Look – your father and I have been looking for you in agony.'

And he said to them, 'Why were you looking for me? Didn't you know that I had to be on my Father's business [or: 'in my Father's house']?' And they did not understand the word that he had spoken to them.

Luke 2:41-50

Luke ends his account of Jesus' early years with a characteristically dramatic vignette. His parents are presented as observant Jews, going up to Jerusalem on pilgrimage; but a note of suspense is injected into the story when they discover that they have actually lost this child that has been so carefully entrusted to them.

The drama is not just for its own sake, however, but for what it hints about Jesus' future. The Jesus of Luke's Gospel is not about to be easily pinned down; and the child who reacts harshly to 'your father and I' by deliberately redefining his parentage ('my Father'), is the one who is going to 'cause division'.

This is a stark passage to pray over.

The Mysteries of Light

The Baptism of the Lord

And it happened in those days Jesus came from Nazareth of
Galilee and was baptised into the Jordan by John. And
immediately coming up out of the water he saw the heavens
dividing and the Spirit like a dove coming down upon him.
And a voice came out of the heavens: 'You are my Son, the
beloved; in you I have taken pleasure.' And immediately the
Spirit hurls him out into the desert. And he was in the desert
forty days being tested by the Satan, and he was with the
beasts. And the angels began to serve him.

Mark 1:9-13

We may puzzle at this, as perhaps the early Christians did: if Jesus is so superior to John, why did he have to be baptised by him? Mark does not really give us an answer, except that a) Jesus sees the heavens dividing (which means that what happens is God's doing), and the Holy Spirit descending (as John the Baptist had indicated) and b) Jesus is publicly affirmed as God's Son.

The word 'immediately' is a favourite of Mark's, and gives a breathless, urgent quality to Jesus' early ministry. Notice the powerful image of the Spirit 'hurling' Jesus, whom we have heard identified as Son of God, out into the desert. We watch with interest, and we wonder how the story will develop.

What does it mean, to call Jesus God's Beloved Son?

The Miracle at Cana

And on the third day, a wedding took place at Cana of the Galilee. And the mother of Jesus was there. Jesus was also invited, and his disciples, to the wedding, and when the wine ran out, the mother of Jesus says to him, 'They don't have [any] wine.' Jesus says to her, 'What is that to me and you, woman? My hour has not yet come.' His mother says to the servants, 'Whatever he tells you, do [it].' Now there were six stone water-jars standing in that place, in accordance with the purification rites of the Judaeans, going up to two or three measures. Jesus says to them, 'Fill up the water-jars with water.'

And they filled them, right to the top. And he says to them, 'Now draw and take to the master of the feast', and they took it. And when the master of the feast tasted the water, which had become wine, he didn't know where it was from, although the servants who had drawn the water knew, the master of the feast calls the bridegroom and says to him, 'People generally set out the good wine first, and [then] when people are drunk, the inferior. You have kept the good wine till now.'

This first of the signs Jesus did in Cana of Galilee and revealed his glory, and his disciples believed in him. After this he went down to Caphernaum, and his mother and brothers and his disciples, and they remained there for a few days.

John 2:1-12

This is an extraordinary story, and we are invited by it to go deeper into the mystery of Jesus. It starts 'on the third day', and a Christian reader inevitably reads this as a reference to the Resurrection.

Next we notice the conversation between Jesus and his mother. Her observation (it is no more than that) about the lack of wine receives what sounds like a sharp rebuff, except that she does not read it so: 'Whatever he tells you, do it,' she says, confidently, to the servants. Then, and with no apparent effort at all, we discover that we have an enormous quantity (something like 180 gallons!) of the very best wine, to the astonishment of the headwaiter, and no doubt that of the bridegroom also.

The point of the story comes at the end; there is no interest in the miracle as such, only in its function as a 'sign', to reveal his 'glory'. These two words are important for identifying Jesus in the Gospel of John. We notice that 'his disciples believed in him'; but the same is not said of his mother, presumably because she was already a believer.

The Proclamation of the Kingdom

Now after John had been handed over, Jesus came to Galilee proclaiming the good news of God and saying, 'The right-time has been fulfilled and the kingdom of God has drawn near. Repent and believe in the good news.'

Mark 1:14-15

Note the starkness of this: the moment when the mission begins is the moment of the arrest of the 'Forerunner'. There is great urgency in Jesus' proclamation: it is now that a decision is required. Like John, Jesus tells his hearers that they must repent, but he also tells them to 'believe the good news'.

Seeing the crowds, he went up into the mountain; and when he sat down, his disciples came to him. And opening his mouth, he began to teach them, saying:

'Congratulations to the poor in spirit –
theirs is the kingdom of heaven.

Congratulations to those who are mourning –
they shall be consoled.

Congratulations to the gentle –
they shall inherit the earth.

Congratulations to those who are hungry and thirsty
for righteousness – they shall be satisfied.

Congratulations to the merciful –
they shall be mercied.

Congratulations to the pure in heart –
they shall see God.

Congratulations to those who create peace –
they shall be called children of God.

Congratulations to those who are persecuted because of
righteousness – theirs is the kingdom of heaven.

Congratulations to you when they reproach you and persecute you and falsely talk all kinds of evil against you because of me. Rejoice, and be glad, because your reward in heaven is huge. You see, that's how they persecuted the prophets before you.'

Matthew 5:1-12

Matthew starts the Sermon on the Mount, the greatest of his five 'sermons' by making sure that our attention is focused. Jesus goes up the mountain, apparently because of the crowds. This reminds us of Moses, except that Moses went up a mountain to receive the Law, Jesus to give a new Law. Then we watch as he adopts the teacher's position ('he sat down'); his disciples join him, and Matthew next offers no less than three expressions to indicate that Jesus is talking: 'he opened his mouth', 'he began to teach', and 'saying'. So we know that we are privileged to hear what was intended mainly for the inner group of 'Jesus' disciples'. We are not prepared, however, for the shock that follows, this astonishing list of those who are congratulated: the destitute, the sad, the meek, those concerned for justice, the merciful, those who concentrate exclusively on God, those who refuse to go the road of violence, those who are persecuted. At first blush this sounds absurd: are Christians supposed to be wimps? But on a second reading (try it), there is a profound wisdom in what Jesus offers, quite the opposite of the congratulations that people normally offer one another. We should reflect thoughtfully on this, and meditate on what kind of a kingdom it is that is being proclaimed.

The Transfiguration

And six days later Jesus takes aside Peter and James and John
and carries them up to a high mountain privately, on their own.
And he was transformed before them, and his garments
became radiant, very white such as a bleacher on earth could
not so whiten [them]. And there appeared to them Elijah with
Moses; and they were talking together with Jesus. And Peter
responded and says to Jesus, 'Rabbi, it is good for us to be
here. And let's make three tents, one for you, and one for
Moses and one for Elijah.'

For he had no idea how to respond. For they became terrified.
And there came a cloud overshadowing them; and there came
a voice from the cloud, 'This is my Son, the beloved. Listen
to him.'

And suddenly, looking round, they no longer saw anybody,
except Jesus, on his own, with them.

And as they came down out of the mountain, he instructed them
that they should narrate to nobody what they had seen, except
when the Son of Man should be risen from the dead. And they
hung on to the message for themselves, arguing what 'rising
from the dead' was. And they interrogated him, saying, 'The
scribes say that Elijah has to come first.' And he said to them,
'Elijah indeed comes first, and restores everything. And how is
it written about the Son of Man that he should suffer a great

deal and be treated with contempt? But I tell you that Elijah has come, and they did to him as they pleased, as it is written about him.'

Mark 9:2-13

The instruction of the disciples goes on, although here it is only his 'inner cabinet', Peter, James and John, who are given their instructions. Up the mountain, two things happen: first, Jesus is 'transfigured', and whatever we make of this, it is clearly intended as a glimpse of the truth about him. Second, Jesus is seen chatting with Elijah and Moses, the Prophets and the Law, so that he is at least the equal of them. Then Peter blows it, with his willing but not very sensible suggestion of building a camping-site. Notice that 'they became terrified'. This is the sign of the presence of God; and, sure enough, there is a cloud and the voice of God, confirming what we heard at the Baptism (1:11), 'This is my Son, the beloved', with the instruction (which they will do well to observe), 'listen to him'.

With these words ringing in their ears they go down the mountain. Then they (and we) are told that this can't be understood until Jesus is raised from the dead, and are invited to think about Elijah. But they don't really understand very much.

We should gaze at Jesus here, and ask to glimpse the truth about him.

The Institution of the Eucharist

And as they were eating, he took bread, blessed, broke, and gave it to them, and said, 'Take, this is my body.' And he took a cup and gave thanks, and gave it to them. And they all drank of it. And he said to them, 'This is my blood of the covenant. It is poured out for many. Amen I tell you that no way any longer shall I drink of the fruit of the vine until that day when I drink it new in the kingdom of God.'

Mark 14:22-25

With Jesus and the disciples, we attend the Passover meal. This is the greatest and most joyous meal of the Jewish year, but it will all end in sadness and betrayal. Jesus starts the meal by predicting that one of his fellow-diners will betray him. And the mood does not lift very much as he takes the bread and wine and says, 'This is my body . . . this is my blood of the covenant. It is poured out for many.' Whatever else this means, it sounds like death. And yet the Eucharist has been an unimaginably precious gift to Christians down the ages. Why? Only because of God's raising of Jesus.

For I received from the Lord, what I also passed on to you, that the Lord Jesus, on the night when he was handed over, took bread, and, giving thanks, broke it and said, 'This is my body, which is for you: do this in memory of me.'

Likewise, the cup, after supper: 'This cup is the new covenant in my blood. Do this, as often as you drink it, in memory of me.'

For as often as you eat this bread and drink this cup, you proclaim the Lord's death until he comes.

1 Corinthians 11:23-26

Central to Paul's understanding of what it is to be a Christian community, is the question of unity, especially at the Eucharist. Paul is horrified to hear of the class distinctions that operate at the Corinthians' communion service: some are drunk, and others are starving! As always with Paul, the solution goes back to Jesus, and, in this case, to what he did 'on the night when he was handed over'. It goes back to the extraordinarily weighty significance that Paul (and Christians before and since his time) attached to Jesus' mysterious words and gestures at the Last Supper, 'This is my body . . . This cup is the new covenant in my blood'. Whatever the precise meaning of this formula, it is not something to be treated lightly.

The Sorrowful Mysteries

The Agony in the Garden

Then Jesus came with them to a place called Gethsemani, and he says to his disciples, 'Sit here, while I go there and pray.' And he took along Peter and the two sons of Zebedee, and began to be sad and to be distressed. And he says to them, 'My soul is very sad, even to the point of death. Stay here, and stay awake with me.' And he went a little bit further, and fell on his face, praying, 'My Father, if it is possible, let this cup pass [me] by; nevertheless [don't let it be] in accordance with what I want, but [with] what you want.' And he comes to the disciples and finds them sleeping, and he says to Peter, 'So you weren't even strong enough to stay awake with me for a single hour!

Stay awake, and pray, that you may not enter into temptation. The spirit is eager, but the flesh is weak.' Again he went off a second time and prayed, 'Father, if it is not possible for this [cup] to pass by unless I drink it, may your will be done.' And again he came and found them sleeping, for their eyes were heavy [with sleep]. And he left them again, and went off and prayed for a third time, again saying the same prayer. Then he comes to his disciples and says, 'Go on sleeping now, and have a rest. Look! The hour has come near, and the Son of Man is being betrayed into the hands of sinners. Up you get – let's go! Look! My betrayer has come near.'

Matthew 26:36-46

This little episode presents us with a Jesus who is doing what he has always told his disciples to do, namely entrust everything to his Father. This whole episode presents us with the meaning of the third petition of Matthew's version of the Lord's Prayer ('may your will be done'), which is quoted here.

Here, as so often, Matthew's Gospel uses contrast to draw Jesus' portrait. In this case, the contrast is between Jesus' own alertness and grief, on the one hand, and the crass somnolence of his disciples on the other.

It is a sad and moving tale.

The Scourging at the Pillar

Now at the feast Pilate used to free for them one prisoner whom they requested. And there was the one known as Barabbas, who had been imprisoned with the revolutionaries who had committed murder in the revolt. And the crowd came up and began to ask [Pilate to do] what he used to do for them. And Pilate responded to them, saying, 'Do you want me to release the "King of the Jews" to you?' For he knew that it was out of spite that the high priests had handed him over. And the high priests incited the crowd that he should rather release Barabbas to them. And Pilate again responded; and he was saying to them, 'So what do you want me to do with the "King of the Jews"?' And they again screamed out, 'Crucify him.' And Pilate tried to say to them, 'Why? What crime has he committed?' And they screamed out all the more, 'Crucify him.'

Then Pilate, wanting to do enough [to please] the crowd, released Barabbas to them. And he handed Jesus over to be crucified, having scourged him.

Mark 15:6-15

The Sanhedrin has held a trial, after which they finally bring the local Roman governor into the matter. Pilate hardly knows what is going on, despairingly asking if Jesus is 'King of the Jews' (about the only concept he can grasp); like the High Priest before him, he gets nothing out of Jesus. Nor, when he tries to release Jesus, does he get anything out

of the crowd (which Mark blames on the high priests).
Everyone seems, on this account, agreed that Jesus has done
nothing to deserve it; but there he is, being scourged in
preparation for a horrible death.

We watch in horror as we see where Jesus' love has
led him.

The Crowning with Thorns

And so then Pilate took Jesus and scourged him. And the
soldiers, weaving a wreath out of thorns, placed it on his head,
and a purple cloak they put round him, and they came to him
and started to say, 'Hail, King of the Judaeans.' And they
rained blows on him. And again Pilate comes out and says to
them, 'Look – I am leading him out to you, that you may know
that I find no grounds [against] him.' And so Jesus came out,
wearing the wreath of thorns and the purple cloak. And he says
to them, 'Behold – the man.' And so when the chief priests and
the servants saw him, they cried out, saying, 'Crucify, crucify.'
Pilate says to them, 'You take him and crucify [him]. For I find
no grounds against him.' And so the Judaeans replied, 'We
have a Law. And according to the Law, he ought to die –
because he appointed himself Son of God.'

John 19:1-7

At this point in the Gospel of John we are coming to the end of a debate between Jesus and Pilate, on the nature of kingship. Pilate can hardly make out what is going on, but is certain that Jesus is a king, and that he is innocent. Nevertheless, in response to the demands of the crowds and of the religious authorities he scourges him as a preparation for execution, and hands him over to the soldiers to play their game of 'King' with him.

Everyone is against Jesus here – are you?

Jesus Carries His Cross

And as they led him away, they took hold of Simon, a Cyrenean, who was coming from the field, and put the cross on him to carry it behind Jesus.

A great crowd of the populace was following him, and also [a crowd] of women, who were mourning him and weeping for him. Jesus turned to the women and said, 'Daughters of Jerusalem, don't be weeping over me. No – weep for your-selves and for your children. Because, look! Days are coming when they will be saying, "Congratulations to the women who are barren, and the wombs that have not given birth, and the breasts that have not suckled." Then they will start saying to the mountains, "Fall on us," and to the hills, "Cover us." Because if

they do these things when the wood is green — what might
happen when it's dry?' And two other criminals were led out
with him to be executed.

Luke 23:26-32

*'And two other criminals were led out with him to be
executed.' Luke has grouped together three groups of
companions for Jesus as he goes out to his execution. The
first and the third are already in Mark, although Luke's
account of Simon of Cyrene is less stark than Mark 15:21.
The second group, however, the 'women of Jerusalem', who
have the courage to show their affection for Jesus, is only in
Luke, and is part of the evidence that makes people want to
call Luke the 'Gospel of women'. Jesus' sensitive response to
their mourning, and the characteristic Lucan note that he
'turned to the women', give the incident great emotional
weight. The line about asking the mountains and the hills to
bury them is already in Hosea 10:8, in the context of the
destruction of the Northern Kingdom. Here it is clearly the
destruction of Jerusalem that is in view.*

*This is a grim passage; we pray over it only because it is not
the end of the story.*

Jesus Dies on the Cross

And when they came to the place that was known as 'Skull', there they crucified him, and the criminals, one on the right, and one on the left. 'When they divided his garments, they threw lots.'

And the crowd stood, watching. And the rulers sneered at him, saying, 'He saved others; let him save himself, if this is the "Messiah of God", the "Chosen One".' And the soldiers who came up also made a game of him, offering him sour wine, and saying, 'If you are the King of the Judaeans, save yourself!' There was also a placard on him, 'This is the King of the Judaeans.'

One of the crucified criminals started blaspheming him, saying, 'Aren't you the Messiah? Save yourself – and us as well!' The other scolded him in response and said, 'Have you no reverence even for God? Because you're under the same sentence; but we deserve it, because we are getting the going rate for what we did. But this man hasn't done anything wrong.' And he said, 'Jesus – remember me when you come into your kingdom.' And he said to him, 'Amen I tell you, today you will be with me in Paradise.'

And it was now about the sixth hour, and a darkness came on all the earth until the ninth hour, because there was an eclipse

of the sun. The veil of the Temple was torn in the middle, and
Jesus cried in a loud voice, 'Father, into your hands I commit my
spirit.' As he said this, he expired.

Luke 23:33-46

*Luke presents three possible reactions to Jesus: the 'popu-
lace' watch; the rulers (familiar Lucan term), soldiers, and
one of his fellow criminals, turn the word 'save' on Jesus, to
show that he's a fake; finally the other criminal gets him
triumphantly and dramatically right, and turns into one of
Jesus' 'terrible friends'. This perceptive murderer asserts that
Jesus is indeed a King (or Messiah) and all but says that he
is God. In addition the reader knows that whatever the rulers
may think, Jesus is indeed 'Messiah of God' and 'Chosen
One'. The episode ends, with arresting solemnity, with
'Amen I tell you' and a striking Lucan 'today', and a most
unexpected conclusion.*

*Luke is still clearly following Mark's account, but he makes
one or two changes, where we can see his hand at work.
He adds the detail about the eclipse of the sun, perhaps
giving a scientific explanation for his educated readers. He
omits Mark's terrible cry of abandonment ('My God, my
God – why have you forsaken me?', Mark 15:34). Jesus'
last words are reported as a much more gentle quotation
from Psalm 31:5.*

We gaze in horror at this terrible ending.

The Glorious Mysteries

The Resurrection

And when the Sabbath was at last over, Mary the Magdalene, and Mary of James, and Salome bought spices in order to come and anoint him. And extremely early on the first of the Sabbaths they come to the tomb. The sun had already risen. And they said to themselves, 'Who will roll away the stone for us from the door of the tomb?' And looking up [or: recovering their sight] they see that the stone has been rolled away. For it was very big. And going into the tomb they saw a young man sitting on the right wearing a white robe. And they were alarmed. But he said to the women, 'Do not be alarmed. You seek Jesus the Nazarene, the one who was crucified. He is risen; he is not here. See the place where they put him. But go, tell his disciples, and Peter, that "he is going before you [or: leading you] into the Galilee. There you will see him, as he said to you".'

Mark 16:1-7

This is a marvellous passage: you can feel the impatience of these women, as they grind their way through the Sabbath, before they can buy spices to do the needful for Jesus' dead body (and notice, by the way, that they evidently did not believe in the Resurrection; you can only anoint dead bodies if they stay where they are put). Mark makes, perhaps, a little joke at their expense, when he says that 'the sun had already risen'; and if the reader is inclined to berate the women for their improvidence in not thinking in advance about how to roll the stone away, then just ask where Jesus' male followers are at this moment. Then there is the young man, and the information that he already has, and the precious proclamation that he gives them: 'he is risen'.

That is the good news that is at the heart of our Christian faith. We rejoice mightily as we contemplate it.

The Ascension

The eleven disciples journeyed to Galilee, to the mountain which Jesus had commanded them. And when they saw him, they worshipped – but they doubted.

And Jesus approached and spoke to them, 'All authority in heaven and on earth is given to me. So go and make disciples of all the Gentiles, baptising them in the name of the Father, and of the Son and of the Holy Spirit, teaching them to keep everything that I have commanded you. And look! I am with you all the days, up to the consummation of the age.'

Matthew 28:16-20

As he said these things, while they looked, he was lifted up, and a cloud took him up, out of their sight. As they were gazing intently into heaven, while he journeyed, look! Two men were in their presence, in white clothes; and these men said, 'Men of Galilee, why do you stand looking into heaven? This Jesus, who was taken up from you into heaven, so he will come in [just the same] way you see him journeying into heaven.'

Acts 1:9-11

The first of these two passages is a powerful scene with which to conclude Matthew's remarkable Gospel. Notice that the disciples are eleven now, a reminder that one of his intimates had betrayed Jesus and then committed suicide.

They go to Galilee, as instructed, and to 'the mountain', a location which, though vague enough in itself, has been important throughout this Gospel.

The disciples show the correct response: 'they worshipped', a gesture first performed (in Matthew's Gospel) by the Magi; but, like all disciples down the ages, they are a bit unsure: 'they doubted'.

Then we are given a further clue to Jesus' identity: 'all authority in heaven and on earth' is given to him, which is a very grand claim indeed. And this leads directly into the mission to the Gentiles: 'make disciples of them', says Jesus, using a favourite word of Matthew's. And they are to baptise these Gentiles in the triune name of Father, Son and Holy Spirit (we may perhaps hear in these words a fragment of the liturgy of Matthew's church) and pass on everything that Jesus taught them (in the Sermon on the Mount, for example). Finally comes the promise, picking up the reference to Emmanuel in Chapter 1, and to the Church in Chapter 18, 'I am with you'. It is only on the supposition of that unfailing and faithful presence that Matthew can write a Gospel at all.

It is clear that the disciples do not really understand at present; this incomprehension continues a theme from the Gospel. That will change when 'the Holy Spirit comes on them'; in a sense, Acts is the working out of this promise. Acts also shows how the apostles became Jesus' 'witnesses in Jerusalem and in all Judaea and Samaria'.

Now they are on their own (only, of course, as the next mystery shows, they are not).

The Coming of the Holy Spirit

At the fulfilment of the day of Pentecost they were all together in the same place. Suddenly there came from heaven a sound, as of a violent wind rushing, and it filled the whole house where they were sitting, and divided tongues, as if of fire, appeared to them, and sat on each single one of them, and they were all filled with the Holy Spirit, and they began to speak in different languages, as the Spirit granted them to utter.

There were Jews living in Jerusalem, devout men from all the nations under heaven. When this sound happened, the crowd came together and were confused, because each one of them heard them speaking in their own language. They were astounded and amazed, saying, 'Look! All these people who are speaking, aren't they Galileans? How do we each hear in our own language in which we were born? Parthians and Medes and Elamites and those who dwell in Mesopotamia, and Judaea and Cappadocia, Pontus and Asia, Phrygia and Pamphylia, Egypt and the parts of Libya round Cyrene, and Roman visitors, both Jews and proselytes, Cretans and Arabs, we hear them speaking in our [own] languages the great things of God.

They were all amazed, and greatly perplexed, one saying to another, 'What's all this about?' But others said, mockingly, 'They are full of sweet [wine].'

Acts 2:1-13

Here we 'see' the Spirit in action, with sound and sights (mighty wind, tongues of fire); we are meant to recall Jesus' baptism at Luke 3:22, with its own sound and sight (the Holy Spirit in bodily form, and the voice from heaven). The fire and mighty wind are symbols of what can be seen in the rest of Acts, as the story of the Holy Spirit unfolds. The 'violent wind' blows throughout Acts, driving the story on, powerfully changing people's lives, driving Saul and Peter and the rest of them on the journey to the 'ends of the earth'; you can see it in the way intense opposition is overcome, in the signs and wonders and healings that accompany the Gospel. 'Tongues of fire' stand as a symbol for the speeches that constitute one third of Acts of the Apostles. See how on that first Pentecost the Gospel was preached to 'all the world', how the apostles cannot be prevented from speaking of Jesus to everyone they meet. Acts is the dramatic illustration of how the fire of the Gospel spread round the Mediterranean world, of how the wind blew from Jerusalem to Rome, and then onwards down the centuries and across the world to wherever you are reading these words today.

Notice how the good news is already reaching 'to the end of the earth', and look at a map for all the places mentioned, to see how it makes a great circle round the Ancient Near East.

The theme of initial rejection or mockery (in this case the allegation that the speakers are drunk) reappears *frequently in Acts. It is part of the energy of the Spirit that it arouses opposition as well as driving the story and the Gospel forcibly onwards.*

Watch this episode unfold before your eyes, and watch out for the Spirit at work in your own life.

The Assumption of Our Lady into Heaven

Look! I am telling you a mystery. We shall not all fall asleep; but we shall all be changed, in a nanosecond, in the blink of an eye – at the final trumpet.

For the trumpet will signal – and then the dead shall be raised undecayed. And for ourselves, we shall be changed. For this decaying part must put on un-decay, and this mortal part put on immortality. But when this decaying part puts on un-decay, and this mortal part puts on immortality, then the word of Scripture will come true: 'Death has been swallowed up into victory' (Isaiah 25:8). 'Where, death, is [your] victory? Where, death, is your sting?' (Hosea 13:14).

The sting of death is sin; and the power of sin is the law. Thanks be to God who gives us the victory through our Lord Jesus Christ!

1 Corinthians 15:51-57

*It is hard to find a good Scripture passage for our doctrine
of the Assumption; but this extract from Paul's insistence on
the doctrine of Resurrection to his restless Corinthians is the
second reading for the feast, and will do quite well. The key
fact is, as Paul makes clear, that God in Jesus has conquered
death, and not just for Jesus but also for us. And it is a very
ancient Christian belief that Mary, the woman who gave
God flesh, who is properly called 'Mother of God' was
herself spared, as a gracious gift from her Son, not from
death, but from death's corruption. Certainly it is a
significant and striking fact that no city has ever laid claim
to the bones of Our Lady. As we pray on this mystery, we
should rejoice at God's victory over death.*

The Coronation of Our Lady
and the Glory of All the Saints

After this I saw, and look! A huge crowd, whom no one could
number, from every nation and tribe and people and language
standing before the throne and before the Lamb, wearing white
robes, and with palms in their hands, and they cry out in a loud
voice, saying,

> 'Victory to our God who sits on the throne,
> and to the Lamb.'

And all the angels stood in a circle [round] the throne and the elders and the four animals, and they fell down on their faces before the throne, and they worshipped God, saying,

'Amen! Blessing and glory and wisdom
and thanksgiving
and honour and power and strength
to our God for ever and ever. Amen.'

Revelation 7:9-12

The final mystery of the Rosary is our story; first it is the story of Mary, best of the human race, and then it is our story. At the beginning of the Rosary, we watched in awe as Mary said 'Yes' to the angel's invitation. Now we watch as all redeemed humanity together celebrates the victory of God.

First published in 2007 by

KEVIN MAYHEW LTD

Buxhall, Stowmarket, Suffolk, IP14 3BW

E-mail: info@kevinmayhewltd.com
Website:www.kevinmayhew.com

9 8 7 6 5 4 3 2 1 0

ISBN 978 1 84417 742 4

Catalogue No 1500991

Designed by Chris Coe
Title pages and page 4 image © Piotr Sikora – FOTOLIA
Pages 3, 21 image © Copyright Evgeny E. Kuklev, 2006.
Used under licence from Shutterstock, Inc
Page 31 image © Richard Kane – FOTOLIA

Printed and bound in China